BLACK SAND

ALSO BY EDWARD BAUGH

Poetry

A Tale from the Rainforest (1988)
It Was the Singing (2000)

Criticism and Essays

West Indian Poetry 1900-1970: A Study in Cultural Decolonisation (1971)
Derek Walcott: Memory as Vision (1978)
Chancellor, I Present: A Collection of Convocation Citations (1998)
Derek Walcott (2006)
Frank Collymore: A Biography (2009)

Edited

Critics on Caribbean Literature (1978)
Annotated Edition of Derek Walcott: Another Life (2004)
Selected Poems of Derek Walcott (2007)

Some of these poems first appeared in *Ariel, Artrage, The Arts Journal, Arts Review, Bim, Bim: Arts for the 21ˢᵗ Century, Calabash, Callaloo, Caribbean Quarterly, The Cincinnati Poetry Review, The Dalhousie Review, The Flinders Jubilee Anthology, Focus 1983, The Graham House Review, The Greenfield Review, Jamaica Journal, Jubilation 50, Kunapipi, Kyk-over-al, The Malahat Review, Mississippi Review, Obsidian III, Pacific Quarterly Moana, Pathways, PN Review, Poetry International, Poui, The Sunday Gleaner, The Sunday Observer, The Trinidad and Tobago Review, Washington Square.*

Poems from *A Tale from the Rainforest* (1988) and *It Was the Singing* (2000) appear by kind permission of Sandberry Press.

EDWARD BAUGH

BLACK SAND

NEW AND SELECTED POEMS

*for Gertrud
affectinately,
Eddie
MARCH 19, 2019*

PEEPAL TREE

First published in Great Britain in 2013
Peepal Tree Press Ltd
17 King's Avenue
Leeds LS6 1QS
UK

ISBN 13: 9781845232108

Supported using public funding by
ARTS COUNCIL
ENGLAND

For *Sarah and Catherine*

CONTENTS

New Poems

from *It Was The Singing* (2000)

from *A Tale from the Rainforest* (1988)

NEW POEMS

END POEM

and when that daring song-tower falls,
may goats and children know delight
poking round each rubbled height
and sunlight
strike bright music
from shards of weed-grown walls.

THE COMINGS AND GOINGS OF POEMS

Interviewers ask me how the poems come.
Do they need some special frame
of mind, some auspicious hour
of night, and where? So this one
is to pull out of my hat the next time
some interviewer asks, to say how
in a delicatessen in Silver Spring, Maryland,
manoeuvring the spare ribs and chicken mushroom
with a plastic fork, and sucking a strawberry
smoothie through a plastic straw, comfortably
vacant and anonymous in the goings and comings
of the lunch-time crowd, and in the midst of everything
realizing that a poem that had been stuck
for months now was completing itself
and I couldn't even pinpoint when the flow began
or why; and then, right there, while that one
was coming, this one came, to tell
how the first one had come. And isn't it worth
a poem to explain, how many a time
things come together, without reason or rhyme?

HURRYING ACROSS HILL COUNTRY

Hurrying across hill country to reach
destination before dark, we crested
the last ridge, and there, rising
before us, stretched wide, the shining
rippled sea, horizon at eye level,
the westering sun directly before
us. It was as if there was no reason
we shouldn't shoot straight ahead,
lose ourselves without trace to tell
of our transcendence. The moment passed.
I eased gently down on the brake pedal,
throttled down, winding carefully downhill
to the beach house and night. Still, it will
recur, the moment, the elusive immanent,
the-always-about-to-happen-but-never-quite.

BLACK SAND

If the poem could open itself out and be wide
as this beach of black sand, could absorb
like black sand the sun's heat, and respond
to bright sunlight with refractions of tone,
nuances that glamour would miss, if this
could happen, if the poem could yield
like black sand, if you looked patiently,
polished stones that fit in the palm
of a woman's hand, could be cool as the sand
where the wavelets splash over her feet,
if the poem could be open like this beach to the breeze,
like these trees that have known great winds,
if the poem could be wide and open, like a love
that is larger than desire, larger than fear,
if the poem could be patient and wide as this evening,
this beach of black sand expecting the night
without fear, the moon lifting over the sea,
the largo of sunset spreading over the city
as the jagged, wounding edges of our unworthiness
are worn down by forgiveness, wave after untiring wave...

BLUE HILLS, BLUE HAZE OF MEMORY

Watching Boon and Waugh walk out
to resume on a dream day at Sabina in March
(and Sydney-siders rubbing sleep
out of their eyes at three o'clock
in the morning), memory resumes and reconnects.

At Wentworth Falls we walked briskly
through a cool, crisp morning, our gaze
drawn to the far blue ridges.
It was like walking across the top
of the world. Distance was in our gift.

I could summon continents of memory –
Aritha Van Herk on Ellesmere, imagining
Anna Arkadyevna remembering the blue
haze on the mountains of Switzerland.

Breakfast was warm bread we brought
back from the patisserie, and Blue Mountain
coffee I had brought to this friendship table
from the other side of the world.

We talked of books and whales and cricketing days
at Royal College, Colombo, and how
our childhoods at the far edges of empire
had given us much that we could share.

I have never seen the playing fields
of Eton, but we fashioned our own style.
That night I drifted to sleep in a hand-carved
bed, under a canopy of birds
in the tree of wishful dreams.

When Boon reaches his hundred
the poem is still struggling
to find its form.

THE ACCIDENT

Yes, right at this spot. It was
a damn funny thing, they say:
wide, straight road, bright bright
middle day, not another car in sight.
They find the brains intact
by itself to one side, just like
somebody take it up careful careful
and put by itself to one side-a
the road. Man, was like
the whole island catch sunstroke
that Sunday. Brilliant fellow, I tell you,
Island Scholar, Cambridge, Inner Temple.
Talk bout good-lookin'! Law practice
booming; just build the big-house on The Hill
plus the beach house down by Point –
fête for so every Sunday! And a wife
some people say was brighter than him,
one sweet Guyana gal!

But you know, the people say is God
make it happen, to show them a sign.
They say O.C. was too arrogant,
like him didn't respect even God self.
Was only about a month before,
one day by the beach house, the argument
come round to politics as usual
and liquor oiling tongue, and O.C.
laying down the law bout what
and what not him going do for the country,
when somebody make some feeble joke
that it look like God forget us,
and O.C. slam the table with him glass
and say, "God! Don't tell me bout God.
Is God and the priest screw up this country!"

Then him rock back on him heel
like was judge and jury
before him, and say, "And too besides,
I have more brains than God."

Well sir, you know how this island stay,
how the people love priest. For a second
was like every jack-man feel
like duppy walk over them grave.
Then somebody laugh, nervous like,
and things back to normal again.
But it wasn't the same any more.
Yes, whatever way you take it,
was a damn funny thing, and the people
swear is God make it happen,
to show them a sign.

THE ARRIVAL

That morning as usual,
the mountain-witch birds
practised their beauty
in the secret places
of the high forest.
In tree-shaded pools
the minnows took life
at their ease. The hillsides
were a concert of green.
And then the miracle of
white sails erupting
like whispering thunder
out of the blue.

AT COVENTRY

We were early for the train at Coventry. So,
to kill time, I strolled round the station,
sniffing out Englishness: the pale poetry
of platforms, waiting-room, cafeteria, loo –
decent, bland; the tracks receding
in the distance, the signal lights on red.
Then, spotting a plaque outside the door
to "Information", I went up close to read.
I expected something about the history
of the site, or which neighbourhood nobleman
had declared the station open on what day,
or something about the bombing of the city
in the war. Instead, I was taken off my guard
to find lines from Larkin's "I Remember, I Remember",
telling how, "coming up England" once
"in the cold new year", the train stopped there
and he looked up to find he was at Coventry,
the place where he was born. Then,
"Philip Larkin (1922-
1985), poet and Coventrian."
Just that. I turned slowly, walked
slowly away. The train came, on time,
and we departed Coventry, gathering speed
as we passed the train-spotter with his pad and pen.
Something, like nothing, had happened there.

THE ICE-CREAM MAN

The ice-cream van tinkles down
the avenue at dusk, to the tune of "Home,
home on the range", although no deer
or antelope play in this neck of the upscale
concrete woods. He must have lost
his way, gliding like the graceful white
swan out of a bygone dream time, where
children frolicking on well-kept lawns
rushed out at the sound of his sweet approach.
You can't even see the lawns or gardens
now, only the high, burglar-daunting
walls. Yet you hear the van stop and wait
for a minute or two, then tinkle on
again. The ice-cream man has done
his market research well. His clientele?
The security guards at the gates of the gated
communities which give the avenue its class.
The moral of the story? A sweet tooth
is no respecter of persons.

WHAT'S POETRY FOR?

"So, what would you say that poetry is for?"
Christ, not that again! I'd read the poem
well; I thought it had struck home.
In short, the interview had gone just great,
and then the question: what's poetry for?

I might have quipped, "It's not for anything;
it is itself, the reason for its being."
I might have quoted Milton, "to allay
the perturbations of the mind and set
the affections in right tune." And yet
the power to perturb you can't gainsay.

I could have said, "For making language
surprise itself, and pitch you to
the high, tremulous edge of silence."
I should have said, "For saying 'no,
in thunder'; tell me when to stop."

But, as the poet said, words failed me.
I mouthed well-meaning platitudes,
and then we slunk away, the poem and I,
to nurse our dream of heaven: a place
where no one asks what's poetry for.

SLIGHT AND ORNAMENTAL

("*A few of the poems are, admittedly, slight and ornamental.*"
Reviewer's comment on a book of poems)

That admittedly slight and ornamental
butterfly that flew across the morning
did not interrupt its flight to reason
with me, or otherwise consider matters
topical or theoretical or of consequence.
How it made light of gravity, displaced
such weight of air! Space expanded
to its map of detours and digressions.
Its sun-dance round the lignum vitae
done, it darted zig-zag off
to eavesdrop on the conversations of trees
and the ruminations of street-dogs filing
single-mindedly down the sidewalk.
Last seen, it was a fleck of dazzle
in the eye-corner of the pelican perched
and gently rocking on a fisherman's canoe
off Hellshire beach. It went, subsumed
by sky and silence. But the clamour of its wings
had traced a yellow highlight along
the day's ephemeral urgencies.

THE LIMITATIONS OF POETRY

It was a poem
that brought them together;
now no poem
can heal the hurt.

TO THE EDITOR WHO ASKED ME TO SEND HIM
SOME OF MY BLACK POEMS

Friend, at first I thought
you had exposed me quite,
found out in me a lack:
I had no colour-coded verse!
But then a thought flashed back:
truth is, my poems are so black
they are invisible to even me,
you wouldn't be able to see them
were I to send them;
moreover, what is worse,
their gravity is so intense
that any light that ventures close
to them just disappears; you too
would be forever lost to view;
and so, in consequence,
not wishing to put you
and your safety on the line,
I beg, respectfully, to decline.

A NINETEENTH-CENTURY PORTRAIT

When Mister Robert Scarlett, master
of Cambridge and Druckett plantations, stood
for his portrait, the good man made a point
of having his personal slave-boy, Oliver,
beside him, waist high, holding his game bag,
with which he'd ride to hunt wild hog
and the occasional runaway. At his other side
his favourite dog. How well the boy's
dark visage serves design,
matching the dark of the trees to cast
in relief the pale, proprietorial white.
Those were the good days; they didn't last.
After the slave revolts of 1831
great houses, factories, everything was gone;
only the family tomb remained.
And what of Oliver? History has left
no afterword; a boy in a picture,
a period-piece, on which poets may stretch out a fiction.

AMADOU'S MOTHER

1. Mother Liberty Speaks

Bring me your hungry and your poor
and I will have them gunned down
in their doorways in Brooklyn and the Bronx
at midnight, by young, clean-shaven
Angels of the Law, in Liberty's
holy name. He was only
a nigger. It was fair game.
Forty-one bullets was the measure
of the need to save the town
from fear. They were pissing their pants
as they knelt to fire. Only nineteen
hit their mark, sure sign of terror.
He is free now. I beckoned
and he came. He followed the dream.

2. *Kandiatou Diallo Speaks*

From the start I knew he wasn't really there,
in that courtroom I mean. I mean it wasn't just
that he was the dead one, the one who couldn't tell
his story. The stars of the show were those four
neatly dressed cops in the dock, the boys-next-door,
Miss America's sons, telling how they wept as they begged
him not to die on them, not to taint their hands
with his blood. They have made a desert of my heart.
Nobody wanted to know who Amadou really was.
Only when the person comes and says the truth
will forgiveness come. He was my son.
He was only a boy going home.

MONUMENTAL MAN

George Washington was something of a mystery,
a man hard to read, but everyone agreed
he cut a fine figure: tall, graceful,
magnificent physique, the only flaw
his terrible teeth, which he replaced
with dentures made of ivory and
teeth pulled from the mouths of his slaves.

What startles most, most reassures
is that I can still be discommoded.
I see him, saddle-smart, erect,
I see him flash an ivory smile,
superior man, superior teeth.
At his death he willed that his slaves be freed.

AN OLDER AND A WISER MAN

Memo to myself:
"Make no more elegies.
Do not collaborate with death."
I was young then. Today
I awakened to accept
that when I tell their going
it is then I praise life most.

TELLING THE TIME

At 3 a.m. the old woman gets out of bed,
puts on her Sunday clothes, and proceeds
to walk about the house. Alarmed,
we cry, "Grandma, where you going?
Day don't light yet!" She replies, "The man
coming to take the house." The house is hers;
the mortgage is discharged. But she
knows something we have to learn:
there's always a man coming to repossess,
and he picks his time.

FREEZE WARNING

There's a songbird that sings at my window
And I wait every day for his voice,
The name of that songbird is Heavenly Love
And the song that he sings is "Rejoice!"

(A song my mother taught me)

On the second, deceptive day of Spring,
when, unseasonably cold, but bright,
the forecast, thanks to America-on-Line,
reads, in red, quote, FREEZE
WARNING TONIGHT, my poet-friend,
silver-haired, capricious, sends me
from home a new poem. It recalls
a day when, he too far from home,
some other Spring bounded clear
of Winter, bang on time. The old
angora, testosterone thudding in his balls,
configures young girls at skip-rope,
an older one bellying with hope
and promise – "jig, jiggle, jerk
and jolt", perennial procreation,
"fish, flesh and fowl", the lot.
At which he sighs, "I am afflicted by the sickness
of the country. I have caught the sadness of the land."
Then springs to mind a song my mother
taught me, about a songbird that sings
at my window; and so, still hearkening,
I click "Reply", then type "Rejoice!"

for Ralph Thompson

34

OBITUARY PAGE

I wonder why nobody can't just die anymore.
Is either you "fell asleep", or "made your transition"
or were "called to the Lord", "or passed peacefully
away". You never just die these days. Even
in death they have you posing. "Passed"?
So why him never stop? I was at home!
Well, listen me now: when time come,
just tell them other one them for me: *Mavis dead*.

THE LISTENING DEAD

The dead are better listeners than the living.
The still depth of their understanding
is not disturbed by any need to reply.
The confidences and questions we bring them
are not disturbed by trying to second guess.

My brother is dying. I find myself speaking
to my father now thirty-five years dead,
who loved him with surpassing forbearance.
"Dad, he isn't going to make it, you know."
The silence settles. Accepts. There is comfort.

THE DARK HOLE IN THE GARDEN

We visit our newly widowed friend.
Just like other times – the familiar
patio overlooking the garden he planted,
his handiwork, his joy; it flowers bright
praise in the Sunday morning sunlight.
We enjoy our usual good spirits,
gin and tonic, Scotch on the rocks.
He never touched the hard stuff,
we chuckle, making cool, playing the bluff.

But there's this dark hole in the garden.
Our talk steps precariously round it,
camouflages it with colour. Sometimes we forget
it is there. Hardest to endure
is the feeling no one dares utter:

that, any moment now, he will walk through the door.

"WHEN THE DOOMED ARE MOST ELOQUENT
IN THEIR SINKING"
(Malcolm Lowry)

He was wired to self-destruct.
Infiltrated by that terrorist dread,
he danced with fierce angels.
His wrists opened, he bled

poems, and the pity of life.
When he cried to us for help
we did what we could, but none of us
could claim success. Instead

we watched as, in slow motion,
riven, lightning-struck, he exploded
into epiphanies, into stars.
We still catch, excitedly, the sky-fall.

WALKING TO JERUSALEM

Pressure hold me now, mi child;
but you see like I making it fret me?
I live my life long time,
I thank God, I taking it easy.
All of your grandmother generation suffer
from pressure, but all of them live long.
Kind of pressure I have, doctor say
anybody else done dead long time.
I ever tell you when I used to dive off the big rock
at Little Bay when we was just so-so pickney?
First time you Uncle Maxi see me
him frighten so 'til: "Binnie, what you doing?
"I going tell Mama!" For him know if anything
happen is him going catch it. Was only
boy business with them things those days.
Is me you take after, you know, come turn
big business-lady! When you father meet
in the accident, and him courage cut, and him
just lay down and wait to die, and I had
Grandma Ethel to look after as well, I had
to do something. Never know nothing
about keep shop, but in two twos
Binnie's Boutique was the talk of the town!
Miss Logan use to walk and tell people,
"Mi dear, Binnie open boutique just so
her daughter can wear pretty frock,"
but was only envy she envy me. Yes, I know,
I know that's what you would tell me,
that is me of mi own free choice decide
to pick up meself and come to this place,
but you know how you sister insistent,
and, to tell you the truth, I never believe
I was going for good. I not complaining,
and I would never say Mavis don't treat me well,

39

but, as I tell you, when you can't change a thing,
you just haffi squeeze you foot a-grung
and bear it. I meet nice people here
you know, but everybody live so far
and nobody have any time, and is hard
to make new friend when you reach my age.
Anyway, I don't think is my time yet,
and you know if anything happen you will hear.
Don't worry, I watching the pressure good good;
just taking me time walk to Jerusalem.

HOLY FEVER

Restless
she moved
from church to church
in search of God.

God grant
she's found him now, where
motionless
she lies
beneath the sod.

A LITTLE NIGHT MUSIC

I must have been nine or ten, when,
one night, our neighbour McKenzie, the Indian
(expediency had changed the family name)
drank himself cursing high, and rode
his horse up and down the street outside
our house, waving his revolver at the dark
and daring my father, "mulatto dog",
to step outside. His short-wave radio,
tuned to Delhi, screeched mood-music
for the mad scenario.

             One duppy-dark midnight
he'd shot at someone up his coconut tree,
certain it was our yard-boy, Vincent.
I guess Dad figured he was right:
Vincent was known to have a way
with other people's crops. But McKenzie
was not a good neighbour. The tall, taciturn,
long-armed detective corporal came
knocking at the gate one day, draped
Vincent by the waist and marched him
to the station to be booked. Dad stood bail
and then character witness. Vincent got off.
So McKenzie decided to settle the score.

Dad, chain-smoking, paced the drawing room.
Mother lay in bed. Nobody spoke. Meanwhile,
Vincent, pure Maroon, crouched
behind the aralia by the gate, cradling
the mortar-stick, and waiting for McKenzie.
In my held breath, a yellow-heart breadfruit
falls from the tree behind our house
and splatters loudly as it hits ground.
The horse eventually decided it had had enough

and took McKenzie home to sleep it off.
I finished my homework, then went to bed,
to a nightmare ending with gunshot and "buss" head.

I WISH YOU A LEAF FALLING

I wish you a leaf falling
from the tree of heaven
catching rare angles of light
as it twirls in its fall, ever
so slowly, such music, such
flute notes, such silence
as it brushes your lips
and the turning earth
pauses at their tremble.
You snatch at it
playfully it slips
your fingers and falls
at your feet and is still.
In the fall of a leaf
such ascension.

MEMORIES LIKE COMFORT STONES

Memories like comfort stones picked up on the beach,
like a girl in a bathing suit astride a beach pony,
and the man pulling on his jeans over wet trunks,
like escoveitched parrot fish, and the little Empress,
fine-boned Nubian, beauty self-possessed,
selling mementos of Marcus and Bob,
her abundance of locks wrapped in Africa cloth –
like the brightness of the day, the shot-silk sea,
like nearness, like promise, like thanks.

MY LADY SAYS

1.

My lady says:
"You are my words man
my memory man
my make-me-laugh man;
the birds in my garden turn cartwheels
when they hear you at the gate."

My lady says;
"You can have all my passwords."

2.

My lady says:
"You are my rain man;
it's good when it comes,
but oh, the dry times!"

3.

My lady says:
"Work harder, worry less,
do the thing you have to do,
then pray."

PILOT BOAT

They watched at twilight as the ship slipped
silently round the headland, the pilot boat
snuggled in its lee side, sliding past
the buoys, the little cay in a pool
of sunlight. Her cheek to his hand, they mused
on pilot birds and pilotfish, and how
big ships need little boats
to take them safely through the inshore
treacheries of reefs and shoals and tight
passages, on the poignancy of need and trust,
on pairings and partings and the animals
going into the Ark two by two. As the last
of daylight dimmed out, they watched the pilot boat
turn back to harbour and release the ship
to open sea, and distance widen
between them. They rose. He brushed sand from her jeans.
They walked away from the beach. Across
the harbour, the city lights had begun to come on.

RIVER SONG

In the lowering light of late September
a man and his goats going home across
the river, hop-skipping the river stones;
and the woman, surprised by love, whispering,
"I have learned never to say never."
The evening hushed, waiting.
A late butterfly alighted on a leaf
then danced into the dusk, leaving
a radiance wet with tears.

MISS LADY IS WEEPING

Miss Lady is weeping. Soundlessly.
You wouldn't know unless
you went right up to her and looked
into her face. The tears well upward,
a slow, unstanchable haemorrhage
from a knot of pain just below
her navel. She thinks that she will
sit there, in her favourite chair,
until night falls, until midnight
sounds or doesn't sound.
He will go to her in the midnight.
He will say to her, "I have come,
the cause of your trouble has come.
I will not leave you." Her arms
enclose his shoulders.
Her heaving subsides.

TRUE LOVE

You lament that you will never know
what it is to go to sleep with me
beside you, and wake up in the morning to find
me there. Consider, love, you will
have had the best of me, the passion
and the tenderness that you command;
not have my body's frailties to endure:
hear me break wind, and belch, and snore,
and, after all that, have to love me still.

WORST-CASE SCENARIO

What would be worst of all is if you steeled
your laughter against the playfulness that you
alone knew how to reach, drew
a shutter across those unblemished eyes
so wide, so bright, so open, in which I knew
approval, and the gate to the garden sighed itself shut,
broken-spirited, the sepia allamanda, the jade bower,
the frolicking fish, and I never again knew days
of poinciana yellow, plumbago blue;
only the disconsolate wish that, when I am only
memory, you might one day read this.

OUT OF STOCK

Chile, is like a spite. I wonder
if it happen to you like it happen
to me. Take last week when I go
to buy the bathroom tiles. As soon
as I check the sample-dem, I know
which one I want, the perfect thing,

not one of the other one-dem would suit.
But when I say to the woman, "May I have
so much and so much of that one?" she smile
and say, "Sorry, Miss, out of stock."

Tell me, why them put the goods on display
if them don't have it to sell?
If was me in power, I tell you, I pass
a law against that kind-a thing.

As to man – every time I see a good one,
one that would suit me just right,
when you hear from the shout
answer come back, "Out of stock."

HALF-A HALF-A GIRL

that ear ring
you can't find
is on my mind
— Gerd Stern

She was always losing one earring,
over the years amassed a treasure
trove of singles that languished at home
in the trinket box, since they wouldn't go out
on the town, where most things went in twos.

Free spirit though she was, a single earring
or the odd coupling was not her style.
Harum-scarum, you'd think. Well, not exactly.
It was just that life was an impatient lover
taking her too often off her guard.

One of these days she'd have the gold
melted down to make a pendant
that would haven, self-contained, between her breasts.
If she cried inside, no one knew.
Could joke about her losings too:
"I'm just a half-a half-a girl."

HOME TRUTHS

"Learn how to make your bed, girl,"
Mother used to say. "Learn to
make your bed so your husband wouldn't
leave you." I smile to myself as I furl
and straighten the spread, while my lover
brushes his hair and straightens himself to go,
and I think how Mother would grieve to know,
having grown so adept at making my bed
I have only this to show, this
superlative man, this lover who leaves.

BAY STREET BOY

For the Bay Street boy turned poet-man and houngan,
word wrencher, spirit wrestler, rough-rhythm-rider;
and for fat pudding-and-souse women in corners
of back alleyways on Saturday afternoons. At night,
lissome and light, they'll shake the fat and rattle
the tambourines. And for where his journeys began,
at Round House, Bay Street, backing on to Burke's Beach
where he learned to swim, from where retraced
triangular Atlantic routes. And for felt-hatted men
bent over warri-boards in front of rumshops,
nudging the nickers, figuring the next play,
while he re-configures language into traps
for spirit thieves, back stabbers, con men.
Word-worrier, warrior, restless drummer, play!

SOUNDINGS

(For Kamau Brathwaite)

The woman quietly crying in the row behind me
that night at UCLA in nineteen-eighty-three
as you read, your fingers tapping the beat,
tapping her river-source of pain and release,
and I'm hearing the beat now as a chattel-house woman,
making tough ends meet, hammers an iron
spike into the ground in the open lot
outside my bedroom window in the already sun-hot
morning at Dover Gardens, to tether her one
Bajan black-belly sheep. Your word-sounds
connect them, sound through them, the one
who hears you and weeps a river of love
and the one who has never heard of you, but pounds
her presence into tough earth, connection
of spirits across oceans, across deserts, grounds
of resistance, resilience. The spirits approve.

YABBA

From Twi *ayawá*, an earthen vessel,
dish, bowl, larder, cooking-pot,
a plain, useful object, pleasing
to handle, contentment to the eye.
A mug's comfortable, no-nonsense *there-ness*,
the whimsy of a vase, wide rim-sweep
of a dish, shapes spawned and spun
from his conjurer's hands, startle of turquoise
against earth-brown, deep forest green –
yabba and monkey jar turn fine art
and Ma Lou protégé, the "yabba man",
is master potter, maker, craftsman!
High cheekbones' ebony glaze,
forehead etched with wisdom lines,
slant-steady, patient eyes
by turns frolicsome and austere,
his thumbs like spatulas poised –
he's folded in earth now, but his fingers
feel the wet and cling of clay.

CHOICES

You chose to leave; that's fine by me.
"One's country," John Milton said, "is wherever
it is well with one." You're still my friend.
Is true, poor people catching hell
and the middle class sleeping
with panic button under their pillow;
but when you fly down to visit
and enjoying the old veranda lime
after dinner, don't spend the time
trying so hard to get me to say
you did right, only a loser would stay.
I wouldn't say I would never leave,
but if that's what they calling ambition,
then for now I sticking with love.
River mullet still running in Grandy water,
and the busu soup simmering,
keeping warm 'til you come.

FLIP SIDE

Preparing every day "a face
to meet the faces that we meet",
we sometimes are quite thrown to find
that people recognize us from behind
the identities we carefully compose
undone in full view of the street.

GUINEA-HEN WEED

Clearing a little space, that's
what it's really about, clearing
a little space, and keeping it.
Visitors exclaim: "What a lovely place
you have here!" They see the smooth
expanse of lawn, the bougainvillea topiary,
the razor-straight hedge, the manicured curb-stones;
they don't see the guinea-hen weed, the grin
on its face, sleek and leering from the hedge-line.
Guinea-hen weed is a natural subversive.
It shuns open ground, deploys its covert
strategies in hedges and garden beds,
among the ornamentals round the house.
You can't weed guinea-hen weed. Most
you can do is stub it back with the machete
and that is knee-bending, thigh-burning business.
My neighbour grows a hedge of guinea-hen weed;
alas, poor privet! I guess you could say
that guinea-hen weed and I have reached
a kind of understanding. For now
I have the upper hand. But I don't fool myself.
I know that when I leave this place
guinea-hen weed will take over, for good.

NEARLY

I'd smile to myself, amused,
when some cocksure wanna-be
called up: "I have a hundred
poems. I'd like you to look at them
and tell me how to get them
published as a book." A hundred!
As if the very number was proof
of excellence.
                        Today I smiled
to myself, amused, amazed
to realize that after two
slim volumes and nearly
fifty years, I'd nearly
reached my hundred.

from *It Was the Singing* (2000)

RESPONSIBILITY

I half awaken
to the comforting blur of my mother
pulling on her house-
dress in the half dark

and already the sound of my father
as from muted dream distance
clucking the chickens to corn.

I too some distant morning
shall rise responsibly
to set my house in motion.

Meantime, I pull the covers close
and smile for the pure secret
thrill of it, and ease myself down
into that last, sweet, morning sleep.

JOE WAUGH, ENGINE DRIVER

He was only a name. He rode into town
after nightfall. From the way he made the whistle
wail as he pulled out of Norwich halt
to bring his iron charger charging
sweetly down the homestretch, the townsfolk
could tell, and would say his name like a boast,
like a spell, over their suppers: Joe Waugh.
I imagined him swing himself heavily down
from his eyrie, shake his limbs loose,
acknowledge with a genial grunt the respect
of station hands and handcart boys,
then pile into his old Ford roadster
and hurry to his hilltop house far
out of town. Next morning he was gone
before I awoke, when first light
silhouetted a fisherman's canoe against
the horizon, and the train traced the curve
of the bay. I never knew him. He was
only a name I cannot erase,
though the townsfolk who recited it are dead
and weeds choke the ties, and twilight transfigures
the stained glass windows of the station house
that is now a museum at the end of the line.

SUNDAY AFTERNOON WALKS WITH MY FATHER

The wharf's high rafters that Sunday
afternoon held a cathedral quiet,
the white-breasted devotions of pigeons.
The old bosun shuffled down from his stool,
ushered us through the wicket gate.
My hand in my father's, I walked whisperingly.

In my head the silence vibrates to the raucous
rhythms of loading day, jests and insults
hurled across the clang of tally machines,
the intense knee-dipping canter of the bearers,
a human millipede hurrying the green
bunches into the sure hand of stevedores
who know the secrets of the dark hold,
and the engines shunting, shunting through
the night, coupling and uncoupling boxcars.

Now a wharf rat peeks out of a hole and turns
into a church mouse. We lean against
the bollards and overhear the water
whispering to the piles. The great ropes
lie like gentle serpents coiled in sleep.

This Sunday was to be special. At my father's request
the bosun unlocked the boathouse door,
a side chapel I had not entered before.
The single rowboat rocked content
on its tether; in the bilge the oarlocks lay casually
close. Every pulse beat whispered, "Rest!"

My father said, "Look!" And pointed. At first
I saw only the shimmer of dappled sunlight
until I caught the knack of looking, and, yes,
there, just under the surface, reaching

67

upwards, a great turtle, its caged ocean-
going hulk, the yellowed inverted prow
of a beak. The glazed eye looked past me.
I said nothing. The afternoon held its breath.

In memory's dark green opaque it lolls
and clambers, a dull, heavy, heavy-lidded
perplexity, glimpse of primeval otherness
under the glint and surfaces of weekday
worlds, Sunday's obstinate, slow
disquieting underside, the lap and suck
of black water, the compelling undertow.

THE TOWN THAT HAD KNOWN BETTER DAYS

When Errol Flynn's red *mg* raced
like rumour through our town, scattering
stray dogs and chickens, old rumheads
slid from bar-stools, lurched through swing-doors
blinking into sunlight just in time
to catch the last puff of exhaust smoke.
His pistol started raftsmen spurring
their bamboo horses down the Rio Grande.
Bets and bravado flew in bright air
and marlin leapt, huge arcs of blue.
At school we envied the boy whose father
landed a job as engineer (the level
didn't matter) on board the *Zacca*, which idled
in the haven of our picturesque, ramshackle port
like some exotic migratory sea-bird
resting between oceanic flights,
and we learned to our befuddlement
that Eve (spelt differently, we were relieved
to find) could be a man's name, when one
of the slow, precociously pubescent girls
who giggled at the back of the class, waved
her autograph book in our faces, showing off
what a French boy – her boyfriend, so she said –
a sort of junior cook on the yacht
(I learned *sous-chef* much later), what that
French boy, Yves, had written. But that
was nothing compared to the bush-telegraph's frenzy
when the Wife of the Moment, so it was said, took
an ice-pick to our Girl-Next-Door-Turned-
Hollywood-Would-Be. Sword fight for days!
High, swashbuckling jinks on the low
seas, badder than those Friday nights at the town's
one cinema, when the rude boys who couldn't find
the fare for pit pounded their revenge on the zinc fence.

Then, one day, news flash. Heart stop. Flim cut.
Star-boy dead. The Sea Hawk strike again! And
the place slipped quietly back to its proper
identity: The Town That Had Known Better Days.

PICKING UP THE PIECES

His alabaster egg, his worry stone
it fell and broke in two.
Your worries are over now, they said.
Not true, not true!
He rushed a petition
to the king, but all the king's
horses and all the king's men
were out on another mission,
while the lady who gave him that comfort
stone had gone away
had gone

THE OCEAN WILL NOT BE HURRIED

The ocean will not be hurried
nor the tides of your love.
There is nothing like your delight
when you incline to be delighted:
a moonflower opening on its midnight tree,
its absence is those mornings
when the harbour puts on
its leaden complexion, and the sea
retracts its gusto deeper
than the reach of deep divers.
For even ocean has days
when she must go down
into herself and lock the door
and be ordinary ocean
communing with her common pain,
counting the rusting hulls.
Let her be. Take example
from the pelican and the frigate bird.
In their dealings with the sea
they are not importunate.
And superannuated men will still
stroll pink coral beaches
at first light, and dawn will break
in their eyes when they stumble
on driftwood fables spun
by the secret nightwork of the waves.

SEASONS

You came at just the best time of year:
mild, dry days, pellucid blue,
the hillsides still green
from November rains.
It was as if you already knew
my climate, not as if it was
just the wind that blew you this way.
Your pleasure was so cloudless, so serene
that, fearing I'd have to watch you
put to sea again too soon,
I couldn't tell you yet
about irritable August
or the waywardness of hurricanes.

AUBADE

Yesterday was Christmas. This morning, morning
came quieter than ever to the close.
My wife and daughter are still asleep.
The neighbour's dog is walking the neighbour.
Etta James is singing Billie Holiday:
"The very thought of you". A blue benediction
enfolds the earth, whispers its healing
in the neem tree, the tamarind, the almond.
The outgoingness of everything is so complete
that, for the first time in the twenty-five years
I have lived in this place, a mongoose feels safe
enough to nose himself up on to the patio
and reconnoitre among the potted plants. The stillness
is suffused with sunlight, and the sound of your absence.

YOU EVER NOTICE HOW

after the maximum leader has spoken
the night's last, great, self-same, expected
speech, the faithful start to party
and the Square break away a carnival
of hips and waving arms
rocking to roots reggae boom
from speaker-boxes bigger and more
durable than poor people's houses;
and you ever notice how when that happen
the maximum leader start to look wrong,
grinning obtusely at what he has
let loose, trying to dance
but him can't catch the beat, and
is like the crowd don't need him now
and the camera backing away for
a long shot and him getting lost
in the crowd, and him just look wrong:
a little man who have a plan
that only him one understand
and him just look wrong, the leader
who can't dance the people music?
And is always the same, check me again
tomorrow night, same time, same square,
different set of players, different
colour costume, but the same script,
different maximum, but the same
two left foot that missing the beat.

AT THE ATLANTIS HOTEL, BATHSHEBA

"... this further shore of Africa" (*Derek Walcott*)

Once Lamming at Bathsheba looking eastward
and night rising like a great wave widening
across the slate-grey water. I watched it
overtake a late, lone seabird.
"If you sail due east from here," he said,
"You'll make landfall at Dakar." I felt
imagination weigh anchor under me, entrust
herself to the sable element, and as
we hove clear of the reef, I could still
make out his spume of white hair
leaping, could hear the echo of his voice
returning from the other side of earth
make one with the surf's boom.

OLD TALK, OR WEST INDIAN HISTORY

From Keith Laurence's gracious patio
on Santa Margarita Circular Road
we looked down on St Augustine, the library
in darkness. Beyond, the line of car lights
traced the Butler Highway and beyond
the Plains of Caroni imagining the Ganges.
A BeeWee sunbird, wing weary, homes
to Piarco from island hopping all day
in the sun, from Norman Manley, Muñoz
Marin, Vere Bird, Grantley Adams, which were once
more felicitously Palisadoes, Isla Verde,
Coolidge Field, Seawell. Diminished at this distance
but doggedly a cane fire burns. It has been burning
for three hundred years. In the morning
as usual we shall brush the soot from the tablecloth
and the pillow. A light which illumines
nothing, our laughter breaks on this hillside,
cascades to meet the sound of silvered
steel ascending from a pan yard. Cut
their names in the bark of this verse: Woodville
Marshall, Keith Hunte, Bill and Nora
Mailer, Joy Pilgrim, Laurence, and the bearded
chief reveller at this wake, the onliest raconteur,
Augier, Roy, who would pronounce
the benediction on every late-night lime.
"No, no, we ain't going home, we ain't
leaving, we ain't going home to night."
You never heard the same tale twice.
Augier's Veranda Talk, an archive
of loose leaves scattered up and down
the archipelago, which only the night wind
will research. In the library below us, the books
on their roosts of shelves twitter among themselves
like schoolboys in dormitories after lights out

about the futility of scribes and the passion
for fixing the past. Laurence, in his italic
style, tells a story how at election time
they dug the road up down the hill
to fix it, then dug it up again
to show how they could fix it. History as the Big Fix.
Roy, ex-Royal Air Force gunner,
tells of sorties among sugar-apple vendors
in Kingston's Coronation Market – O
those imperial trades! Now hear this one:
"Paradise is to kotch up with a book, eating
sugar-apple under a sugar-apple tree
and then old Omar Khayyam wouldn't
have nothing over we."
                                        This settles nothing,
fixes nothing. It is only what I remember
and what I made up, what I made. I wanted
something to remember them by, so I invented it.
At dawn the sunbird will lift from Piarco,
a busha bird riding out to count his plantations.
From the height of noon, over Hispaniola
you will look down through a clarity so absolute
it hurts – the brown land after
the denudations of history, the shining caravels
of clouds, each moored precisely over
its shadow, and even earth's hurt-
ling seems to have stopped. But you can't hold
this high, the engines' throb will cut through
any epiphany, always, ladies
and gentlemen, we are about to begin our descent.
Grip the arm-rest and pray: smooth landings
mild evenings and gracious patios.
                                        But man,
how you could ramble so? Yes, I had meant it
to be purposeful, like history; but is only old talk.

LONG SERVICE AWARD

("If labour is so repugnant to the inclinations of mankind in general, it is doubly so to the Negroe in the West Indies..." — A Planter [Edward Long], *Candid Reflections...,* 1776)

They never thought to ask her what she wanted.
They gave her a clock. "Tenk you, sah. It pretty."
When the big boss from foreign shook her hand
it shocked her, to think a big man's hand
could be so pink and soft, softer and pinker
than a white baby's bottom, or the just-born mice
that fell from the ceiling when she was a child.
Her blood still ran cold, remembering. Strange
how it's always a clock or a watch they give you.
Next day you check the shops to see how little
it cost them. But really, it isn't strange, it's only
salt rubbed slowly into the wound of time,
a clock, to count fifty years traversing the cane,
back bent, beaten by sun and rain.
One full-moon night, years ago, she found
herself walking the cane rows, looking for something
she thought she had lost, and trying to figure out
what it was. Tonight she leans on the windowsill
looking out. She hears her invalid daughter
turn in the bed behind her. She sees
the flickering lights in her neighbours' shacks,
she sees shooting stars falling down
the bright November sky, she feels
the greatness of the world move in her
like deep, dull pain.

VIEW FROM THE GEORGE HEADLEY STAND, SABINA

"You see, you see what I tell you,
he playing and missing, I tell you!"

"No, no, you don't read the stroke.
He know what he doing, he leaving
the ball alone. Just at the last
crucial moment, he easing the bat
inside the line and letting it pass."

"Well, all I can say is that that
is a damn dangerous way
to be leaving the ball alone."

"What you saying in truth? You mean
you meaning to tell me in this
almost twenty-first century them white boys
making my boy look fool?"

"Mister man,
all I know is it wrecking my nerves,
for just make that ball swerve
a fraction and follow the bat
and braps is a snick to slips
and, ole massa, we gone, we dead!"

"Cho, I don't care what you call it,
that is what I call a indigenous
stroke. You know what I know?
This argument can't settle, for if
him out now caught in the slips
that still wouldn't prove nutt'n,
and if you ask him himself, the man
would be a fool to tell you the truth."

"Gentlemen, gentlemen, is watch
we come to watch cricket, or is
epistemology we come here to talk?
This chicken sweet, yes? Is Brenda
cook it? Say what? You mad?
You don't know long time that rum
don't agree with my stomach? Man,
just pass me the Scotch."

NIGHTWALKER

When they asked James Meredith
what it was like to be
the first black student at Ole Miss,
he replied: "It's like you walk in the dark
and a bird flutters in the bush.
I have walked in the dark
and the bird is always fluttering."

IT WAS THE SINGING

It was the singing, girl, the singing, it was that
that full my throat and blind my eye
with sunlight. Parson preach good, and didn't
give we no long-metre that day
and Judge Hackett make us laugh to hear
how from schooldays Gertie was a rebel
and everybody proud how Sharon talk
strong about her mother and hold her tears.
But the singing was sermon and lesson and eulogy
and more, and it was only when we raise
"How Great Thou Art" that I really feel
the sadness and the glory, wave after wave.
Daddy Walters draw a bass from somewhere
we never hear him go before, and Maisie
lift a descant and nobody ask her,
but it was the gift they bring, it was
what they had to give and greater
than the paper money overflowing the collection
plate. It was then I know we was people
together, never mind the bad-minded and the carry-down
and I even find it in my heart to forgive
that ungrateful Agnes for everything she do me
and I sing and the feelings swelling in my chest
till I had to stop and swallow hard.
Then sings my soul, my saviour God to thee,
How great thou art, how great thou art …
and we was girls again together, Gertie
and me by the river, and then the singing
was like a wide water, and Gertie laughing
and waving to me from the other side.
Girl, I can't too well describe it.
Was like the singing was bigger than all of we
and making us better than we think we could be,
and all I asking you, girl, is when

my time come to go, don't worry
make no fuss bout pretty coffin
and no long eulogy; just a quiet place
where gunman and drug addict don't haunt,
and if they sing me home like how they sing Gertie
I say thank you Jesus, my soul will sleep in peace.

TIME FRAME

She's sixteen now, and clatters
down the stairs at risk
of limb – the same stairs
where as a toddler for one
long breath-stopped moment
years ago she fell and landed
right side up and smiling.
"Catherine!" we yell at her,
"You'll break your neck! You'll ruin
your slippers again!" You'd think
by now she would have learned
that nice girls move demurely.
Her wide smile disarms me:
"But I can't help it!" Then
it occurs to me to be glad
I shall not be around to see
her take the stairs the way
her grandmother now goes, dragging
one foot to meet the other
in her halting, reluctant descent.

ON BEING MISTAKEN FOR EDDIE BRATHWAITE, THERE
BEING OF COURSE NO SUCH PERSON,
AND WITH APOLOGIES TO J. ALFRED PRUFROCK

No, I am not
Eddie Brathwaite
nor was meant to be
and anyhow
he's Kamau now
while I remain
just plain
Eddie

VISITING PROFESSOR

The sun pops up out of the Pacific
and showers Mt Keira with light.
I grope for my Sony to find out
how things are going with the world
but also to put off hauling
myself up into another day.
Must finish writing the paper
must do my ten minutes' exercise
must shower, must snap, crackle
and pop into action, light-bringer.

This place is called Wollongong.
A few miles up the road is where
Lawrence wrote *Kangaroo*. Yet again
I do the arithmetic to figure out
what time it is at home
and guess what they're doing now.
"You can never guess," says Jim, "the numbers
you'll get for this kind of talk. We should
get ten." I know. Ten would be great.
I have counted my footfalls echoing down post-
colonial corridors. I profess marginalia.

But draw back the curtains. Look.
The blanketed horses are grazing
on the lower slopes as if exactly
as I last saw them at nightfall.
A rosella enhances the morning.
This place is called Wollongong.
A few miles up the coast
is where Lawrence...
Must get back to the paper,
must get back...

HEDGE TRIMMING

In another life I'll let the overgrowth
grow over me, once in a while
not pass the afternoon hedge clipping.
Come to think of it, maybe I'll not
keep a hedge, nor hedge my bets
nor live so much in parenthesis.
I'll study the passions and subtleties of weeds,
make new terms with earth, its terrors.
No longer now the neighbourhood boast
and envy, who once could keep so straight
a line, so spirit level through murrayea
and privet, fastidious worrier at the edges
of things, Blake's "tame high finisher
of paltry blots/ indefinite or paltry rhymes."
Neighbourhood dogs will take back to their mistresses'
drawing rooms reports of strange sightings:
a wild man laughing through the overgrowth.

THE HOUSE

If we had known, that wet October night
when we moved in, if we had known
that twenty-three years later we'd still be here,
no doubt we would have made more shift
to shape the place to our convenience,
contrived more cupboard space, knocked a wall
or two out, extended the patio, shaded
it with an awning, had a powder-room
put in downstairs, to make it more congenial
to a more expansive life. We settled
for less; it was we who made accommodation,
adjusting ourselves to its rigidities,
saying it was not our place, and in any case
we'd soon be gone. Still, it served us
well enough. It held against the hurricane.
You watched as the big glass door bellied in
and held, then straightened itself out again.
It was a good place to come home to, to come
into the always surprising cool of the living room
from out of a hot noon. It was good for the children
to have grown up here. I learned to tell
pea-dove from whitewing, and to admire
the elegant, deadly geometry of the sparrow hawk.
That wet October night, we brought the baby
last, bundled against the damp, wide-eyed
and blinking at the empty, echoing walls.
Tomorrow she will marry. There'll be a marquee
in the garden, and musicians, a pride
of groomsmen, wit and grace and gaiety.
Something, perhaps, will be fulfilled.

JOURNEY

(After Edna Manley's wood carving of the same title)

I go a journey. This bark that bears me
this curving wood my winding sheet
opens and lifts, makes angel wings
about my shoulders. The dark hollows
of my eye sockets, of my cheeks, the empty well
below my rib cage, the cup of my palm
acceptant – these grave concavities.
I am the vessel. Fill me, Lord.

Stripped down for motion, my feet
together, pointing, my body
arcs like sail to wind, like dove-
releasing hand, aspiring. I lie
cradled by these arms of wood hewn
from a tree of love – my boat, my bier.
I go under. I ascend. Draw me, Lord.

TRAVELLING MAN

Man, you travel far. Remember
those days when they praised you
for what they called your simple, native
craft, secure in their belief
it knew its place, colonial backwaters,
ramshackle, picturesque ports?
But craft is craft, and a man
has the pulse of the sea in his wrist
or he doesn't. So when at last
they rose to cheer you, master
mariner, manoeuvring your craft
that had encompassed the world
into that port from which they once sailed
to claim the world, and hailed
you now as man, as craftsman,
I stood in that crowd by the quayside,
the only one not clapping,
and anyone glancing at me
then might say, "But look
this man! Him dead or what?
Him don't see history in the making?"
But my joy was too much for display:
it needed the space of silence.
Why bother to tell them I knew
the place where the journey began,
that you were not alone, that you brought
with you a people, that you had earned
the silence beyond applause?

from *A Tale from the Rainforest* (1988)

THIS POEM

This poem contemplates a time
beyond the consoling agony of words.

I watched my father dying in bitterness,
I held his ankles as the cold crept close.

This poem turns frail eyes on emptiness
and keeps its peace.

I have seen the eyes of girls grow wide and world-illuminant
at smallest gestures of considerate love.

Hearing disorder gather to its thunderous head,
this poem tests its wings
and tunes its throat.

ELEMENTAL

I would have words as tenacious as mules
to bear us, sure-footed
up the mountain of night

to where, at daybreak
we would shake hands with the sun
and breathe the breezes of the farthest ocean

then, as we descended
in sunlight
we would be amazed
to see what hazards we had passed.

IMAGINE

Imagine, beloved, a time before language,
when the word for love had not yet been
conceived, and imagine my hand moving
across darkness to the knowledge that the curve
of your cheek was made to its measure, and waiting,
and no word yet for cheek or hand
or love – only gesture that admits
no ambiguity, only this mute
importunate hand, like a shield
to the flame of your face.

TRUTH AND CONSEQUENCES

When the mob swerved
at him
he screamed
"I'm not the man you're after.
I'm Cinna the poet.
I never meddled in politics!"

The mob knew better. "Then tear him,"
it screamed back, "tear him
for his bad verses!"

It was then he learned
too late
there's no such thing as "*only* literature".
Every line commits you.
Those you thought dead will rise,
accusing. And if you plead
you never meant them,
then feel responsibility
break on you in a sudden sweat
as the beast bears down.

"I AM VERY PROUD, REVENGEFUL, AMBITIOUS"
(*Hamlet to Ophelia*)

Sulking down dank passageways
in the doom-draped castle of his mind,
he met himself attended by three beasts:
Ambition, Pride, Revenge –
an apparition that disturbed him more
than did his father's ghost.

But who would believe him?
What? The Lord Hamlet?
Such a capital chap? Not he
most mild of princes, prince
of humility and the blameless life.

Well, there it was, the challenge flung down,
which audiences would smile at
then ignore –
the truth, so often to be tossed
as if in jest or madness
only to innocents or fools.

GETTING THERE

It not easy to reach where she live.
I mean, is best you have a four-wheel drive,
and like how my patty pan so old
and spare parts hard to get, I fraid.
I wonder why that woman love
hillside so much, and winy-winy
road, when everybody know
she born under Cross Roads clock and grow
by seaside like all the rest of we.
Some part, I tell you, two vehicle can't pass
and if rain falling is watercourse
you navigating, and rockstone mashing up
you muffler, and ten to one
a landslide blocking you. You must
keep you eye sharp for the turn-off
or you pass it and lost. I bet
by now you dying to know
who this woman I talking bout
so much! Well, to tell
the truth, I not too sure
myself. My friend who study
Literature say she is the tenth
Muse. Him say her name
is Silence. I don't know
nothing bout that, but I want
to believe what them other one say
is true — that when you reach
you don't worry so much
bout the gas and the wear-and-tear
no more, and it have some flowers
and bird make your spirit repose
in gladness, and is like
everything make sense, at last.

THE POET BEMUSED

Yesterday I put on
my antic disposition
but it wasn't any use
it didn't at all amuse
her ladyship, I fear
she's making plans to leave me

so I shall return
to the mode taciturn
the man of few words
proverbially un-speaking.
They'll whisper, "He's deep, that one,"
but only her gone
ladyship carries the secret:
"He really had nothing to say
under the silence, least of all
about important topics
like poverty and politics,
why, as you'll note
he never even wrote
a rodney poem. Can you
blame me for leaving
the creep?"

CAPRICORN

That my hand alighting
lightly on your belly
as I leaned to kiss you
could have provoked such trouble,
that I could slip so
easily out of my years
to be the quivering boy again –
these portents, woman,
spell desolation, for
the astrologers have told me
that my soul-mates are gravediggers,
the weakness in everything
leaps immediately to my eyes,
the shadows of endings haunt
all my beginnings; moreover
I was born old; I contain
abandoned places.

THE HOUSE OF POEMS

When I entered your house of poems,
lady, poet, friend,
everything received me easily –
from the cat
who stuck her head
round the corner of the house
as I came down the steps
then proceeded to take me for granted
to the paintings
unselfconsciously askew
and you
leaning against the window
in barefooted ease
lighted by your landscape.

The earth-brown pages
the floorboards of burnished sienna
bore invisibly the imprint
of your defiant stride.
You brought the scent of the country:
mint tea in cups of fragile bone
blessed by the lips of ancestors.
I was filled by your laughter
deep as hurt, I knew
you could not be contained.

And we talked through the afternoon
around untroubled silences
until dusk began to deepen
the repose of old mahogany
and you said: "It's getting dark.
I should put on a light."
And I said, "I'd better go now."

When rainclouds darken over our mountains
my fingers idle through the pages
and I think of a cottage nestled
in the crook of the road's arm
the blessing of friendship
the longsuffering of desire
and the beneficence of your house of poems
lady, poet, friend.

AN OPEN LETTER TO FEELINGS OF INSECURITY

In case you haven't noticed, this letter
is being written in red ink. LEAVE
MY WOMAN ALONE (exclamation mark).
Last night when she came home
I could tell from the droop of her shoulder
over the kitchen sink, and how she refused
even a campari, and smiled wanly
when I tried to make her laugh –
I could tell she'd seen you and gone
all weak-knee'd and wavering.
Don't you remember how well I know you,
your style and strategies, from those days
we shared a bachelor flat? Why is it
we always fell for the same girl?
I thought I had this one sure and
secure to myself and contented,
cared for, respected. Yes, yes, I know
the feminist critics will say, "There,
don't you see he's given it away
with that male chauvinist *had*,
desire to own, control and protect
into domesticity and moon-eye'd zero?"
Well, maybe I put it badly. God knows
I tried. But for old times' sake
man, GET OFF MY BACK. Your pal.

WOMAN, BIRD

"What is that bird?" "A heron,"
she replied before any of the others
at the table had even heard my question.
Her back had been turned to it. There
was no sign she had seen it alight.
She answered as if she had been
wondering when I would ask.
She was delicate, in a slightly
awkward way guardedly watchful.
She could take wing at a careless
remark. She was a poet.
I shall never see her again.

A TALE FROM THE RAINFOREST

The bird flew out of the rainforest.
It was a day like any other, or so it seemed
until the poet at his desk looked up and saw
the marvellous omen hovering
by his window, shedding radiance.
Then shyly, shyly, yet as if compelled
it entered and alighted
its eye dilating in terror
its head inclined.
The poet rose and moved towards it.
His hand shook to close around
the warmth and tremor of its breast,
such trust, such expectation.
"I too am a poet," whispered the bird,
"My sister the rivermaid sent me.
She told me you would be kind.
The grief of the rainforest
is sometimes hard to bear
and I have had such dreams."
The poet took up his quill,
it became a flute.
They made music
together until
the rivermaid called time
and the nameless bird
flew back to the rainforest
to its midnight of moonflowers
and fern-fringed pools
its nest at the centre of grief.

RUNNING RIVER WATER

I see you by rivers and big-leaved trees.
I dip my hands in running river water
and cool the throbbing of your temples.
I am honoured by the occasions
when your eyelids flutter
like frightened birds.

Deep river woman
you bear, like a covenant,
the memory of mountain huts and yam hills,
the kreng-kreng full and savoury
against hard times, you whisper
like beatitudes the unwritten histories
of flight and ambush and survival.

Woman river
I dip my hands
in running river water
and say: run free
run free

THE WARNER-WOMAN

The morning shimmers in its bowl of blue crystal.
Me, underneath my mother's bed,
I delight in dust and dimness.
Connoisseur of comics and the coolness of floorboards,
I prolong my life's long morning.

But the blue sky broke. The warner-woman.
Bell-mouthed and biblical
she trumpeted out of the hills,
prophet of doom, prophet of God,
breeze-blow and earthquake,
tidal wave and flood.

I crouched, I cowered, I remembered Port Royal.
I could see the waters of East Harbour rise,
I saw them heave Caneside bridge. Dear God,
don't make me die, not now, not yet!

Well, the sky regained its blue composure.
Day wound slowly down to darkness.
Lunch-time came, then supper-time,
then dream-time and forgetting.
Haven't heard a warner-woman
these thirty-odd years.

COLD COMFORT

This a.m.: read a new Larkin
poem – "Aubade" – had
the authentic shivers, gooseflesh.
Then started worrying about how
supposedly death poems and
love poems are luxuries
we in the third world
cannot afford. But
this was one cynic
who couldn't afford
to ruin his day, so
sucked my teeth – bowed
again to the page – shivered
again for the brothers,
first, second, third
and otherwise,
not to mention myself,
transfixed by the steel-grey light
of that bone-chilling, bleak aubade.

INGRID BERGMAN'S HAT-BRIM
AT THE END OF CASABLANCA

It can come from anywhere, unobtrusive,
exact, the line that holds everything
together, the line that was lying

in wait for the poem. As in those
closing frames of *Casablanca* – the lights
glowing wanly out of the night-

fog, the propellers beating, beating,
the stoical, desperate heart, and
especially the fine diagonal

of Bergman's hat-brim across the oval
of her face. It balances everything,
its certainty against the obscuring

mist; the twin astonishments
of love and loss that light her face;
the weight of the tears that refuse to fall –

the line that closes an epoch, that
encloses the one grief of the world.

for Neville and Mysser Hall

INSTAMATIC

And here's Catherine
at sixteen months
barely above ground
and yet
so sky-inclined
Daddy, hustling, must yield
to her insistent "Bird! Bird!"
or "Plane!" or
"Moon!" – her innocence
sanctifies
object and word.

She grows fast
like us to hustle time
to lose
her skywardness.

YARD-BOY

He wielded my boyworld
on his Charles Atlas shoulders,
I the skinny weakling
named "Before", on the covers
of those comic books
he couldn't read.
I told my days
by the strokes of the axe,
morning after morning,
the haft seasoned
by the sweat of his palms,
the blade flashing, splitting
wood for the dover stove.
Sundays he rested
and polished our shoes.

And I polish these words
from which nothing
accrues to him;
and yet, wherever he may be,
these words are hands laid
lightly on shoulders
that hefted so much,
and this, I insist,
is a tribute.

FOR SIMON COLE

sculptor in alabaster
late of Kintyre
who died leaving Athlene
and seven children.

Hardly knew the man –
small, alert, decorous –
but I had seen some of his pieces
and had been making promises
to myself: I'd buy
when things got better, I'd
go to see him where he carved.

Now all I may manage
is this remembrance
which longs
to be as quiet and definitive
as the one piece I had bought –
a bud vase, it stands
on a high bookcase, above eye level,
you'd hardly notice it
against the wall's dead yellow;

but it holds itself
assuredly, serene,
a vase that needs no flower to complete it,
unmarked, unsigned,
its only adornment
the discreet exuberance of the stone.

JUNE ROSES

Flo, Floris, flower of Eden,
my aunt who died young
(her face framed in curls
as how, at Boundbrook,
June roses framed our house)
and sometimes when she laughed
her pleasure overflowed
in tears that sparkled.

In the studio photograph
she holds me, cheek against her cheek
(as Mr Hyde disappears
under his black, magician's cloth).
Then suddenly, insouciant,
blithe, she left – gone
to spend time with relatives
she'd never met. Not to worry,
she'd be back soon, to play
little mother again.

Next memory: my mother in childbed,
the telegram frozen to her hand.
I overheard whisperings
knew I shouldn't ask
how, why she died.

June roses heavy with raindrops.
Black curls wreathe her smile.
Where our house stood
is an empty lot.

WORDS

My mother loved words. Not necessarily
in sentences or speeches. Just words.
She read the dictionary like a bedside book.
She taught me words while I watched her
at the crossword puzzle, her relief
from drudgery. And now this
delectable, mouth-filling word
I cannot teach her: *metastases*,
"multiple metastases". The word
glows a guilty secret through
the large brown envelope lying on
the back seat with the x-rays and
the radiologist's report. She sits
rigid with pain, too proud to ask
if there is any word of relief.
In the silence between us
you can hear the metastases multiply.

AN AGEING LADY

You'd never think
seeing her step so prim
and whalebone-straight to church,
dropping like scented handkerchiefs,
now here, now there, a smile —
you'd never think
so much calamity licked at her heels.

Her God had blessed her womb:
six children were her harvest gift.
Raised them to her image of prissy perfection,
testaments of virtue for the tongue-wagging town.
The blight, when it revealed itself, was cruel.

Two long since are mad,
and one of those her only son.
Two others, fragile spinsters, whose
pale, proud hands have known
no toil or tenderness,
flutter on the edge of the abyss.
The other two — a tale of bitter marriages.

Watch her now
this Harvest Sunday morning
sidle splendidly and late into her pew,
attended by her ghostly retinue
of spinster daughters.
She turns to ask the number of the hymn,
then, aiming at the rafters a youthful vibrato,
outworships her neighbours and magnifies her Lord.

On arch and altar-rail the offerings bloom.

SMALL-TOWN STORY

What of the wives they envisioned then,
when, after cricket and cowboys, they sat
in the veranda's dark and swopped
their chaste, pre-adolescent dreams,
in rivalry of mannish chat
foretelling splendours of domestic bliss?

Beautiful those dream-wives, rich,
and (down, sneaking prejudice!)
fair-hued, if I recall. Too soon
too soon their tongues discovered "bitch".
They leapt too soon to manhood; too late
they lingered in the stagnant town.
The ships came in, the ships went out,
they watched romance and vision drown,
then turned from gazing at the sea
to win their spurs and battle-sores
on randy, sailor-ridden whores.
Woman was sweeter than ever they dreamed
and a stickier jam-pot for eager flies;
now screaming kids with snotty noses,
now debts and escalating lies.
Reality is rum and puke
and endless, pointless noons to grieve,
and a plain, fat woman to deceive.

To such a saga I return
some any-ordinary day,
I who, as the townsfolk say,
"made good", "got education".
But what will books and rhetoric
avail, which raise no bridge of words
to span the graceless silences
that swell between us now, no trick

to cheat the disenchanted gaze?
Lectern-glib, tuxedo-smooth
at after-dinner speech, I find
no word for mates with whom I roared
the sun to sleep in june-plum days.

Now, thanks to booze and boorishnesss,
they do not grace my wedding feast.

THE CARPENTER'S COMPLAINT

Now you think that is right, sah? Talk the truth.
The man was mi friend. *I* build it. *I*
build the house that him live in; but now
that him dead, that mawga-foot bwoy, him son,
come say him want a nice job for the coffin,
so him give it to *Mister* Belnavis to make –
that big-belly crook who don't know him arse
from a chisel, but because him is big-shot, because
him make big-shot coffin, fi-him coffin must better
than mine! Bwoy, it hot me, it hot me
for true. Fix we a nex' one, Miss Fergie.
That man coulda knock back him waters, you know sah!
I remember the day in this said-same bar
when him drink Old Brown and Coxs'n into
the ground, then stand up straight as a plumbline
and keel him felt hat on him head and walk
home cool, cool, cool. Dem was water bird, brother!
Funeral? *Me*, sah? That bwoy have to learn
that a man have him pride. But bless mi days!
Good enough to make the house that him live in,
but not good enough to make him coffin!
I woulda do it for nutt'n, for nutt'n! The man
was me friend. Damn mawga-foot bwoy,
is university turn him fool. I tell you,
it burn me, it burn me for true!

THE PULPIT EULOGISTS OF FRANK WORRELL

They should have talked of cut and glance,
described the dance
he did on such or such a day
on what green floor
on what astonished field.

Instead, they said he was a gentle man,
praised him as a model for his race,
noted with what aplomb he took his place
as senator; a leader cherished
by his men, in friendship steadfast,
who, in spite of bitter recollection,
loved his country at the last.

Any clown can play the gentleman.
But who could time a ball so sweetly
or flick a wrist so strong so featly?
Yet those who saw him in his day
have left the middled things to say –
the strokes, the swing, the easy stance.

But I lay you odds (all death's a game)
that the God to whom they commend his name,
that God remembers cut and glance,
designed, who knows, the deadly dance.

PEOPLE POEM (THE LEADER SPEAKS)

In the name of the people
I give you the People's Constitution
in which the rights of the people
have been enshrined.
So now that the people's rights
are enshrined, meaning dead,
let us get on with the business
of building the nation
for the good of the people.
But remember: be vigilant.
Anybody who trouble me trouble you
for *you* is *me*; *I* am the people –
in the name of the people
and the people
and the people

TURNING POINT

The road meanders through
the late lackadaisical Saturday afternoon.
We follow it, exploring. Weekend conquistadors.
My friend is showing me the island.
The centre of it is round here somewhere.
After the last, crippled signpost, we drive past
ruined groves of blotched carbuncular cocoa
trees and senile, bearded citrus. Then
the road stops. Just like that.
Just bush and a footpath losing itself
off to the left. Only the map tells us
the name of this place. *Mundo Nuevo!*
Some joker must have named it: new world,
dead end.
        So, that was it.
At least we could say we'd been
to the heart of the island.
We turn round, head back to town,
talk of other things, as shadows overtake
that desolation. But *Mundo Nuevo* nags.
Did the metaphor disturb a sleeping nerve?
Perhaps it wasn't a joke. Perhaps
that moment when he named it
marked a promise, or possibility,
a turning point, some final resting-ground
at lonely journey's end.

COUNTRY DANCE

Those country folk dancing a *schottische*
to shac-shac and fiddle in the one-room
schoolhouse-cum-village hall
are not concerned with origins.
Miss Bibsy leads, rakish
in Sam's battered fedora.
Unstaid her sweep and bounce
of buttock. Read Africa.

We had come seeking the true folk
the immaculate idea untouched by irony,
and what could be truer than Bibsy's
callused heel stamping its assurance
on this hard ground?
Night, rolling in from the Atlantic,
washes over the island
re-enacting migrations.

The sea's complaint is the sigh of the tides.
And in the pause between two breakers
was that a skirl of bagpipes?
Doan worry bout that, Sammy boy,
Scotlan' is a district in Barbados
from where, on a clear day, if you eye clean
you can make believe you seein' the golden shores.

Night, rolling in from the Atlantic,
washes over the island.
Later, picking my way
down the hill
in the dark
the music bounces in my head
like light.

COLOUR SCHEME

The rainbow is the shape of God's desire:
all colours bend together, blend,
arching from end to end of earth,
curve of love and loveliness.

That's only a deception for the eye.
Skin-deep excuses are enough
to make a Memphis of the world.

The rainbow fades and aspirations die,
one red encroaches on the sky.
The rainbow, sign of God's desire,
is earnest of the final fire.

NIGGER SWEAT

'Please have your passport and all documents out and ready for your interview. Kindly keep them dry.' (Notice in the waiting room of the US Embassy, Visa Section, Kingston, 1982)

No disrespect, mi boss,
just honest nigger sweat;
well, almost, for is true
some of we trying to fool you
so we can lose weself
on the Double R ranch
to find a little life.
But, boss, is hard times
make it, and not because
black people born wutliss;
so, boss, excuse this nigger sweat.
And I know that you know it
as good as me,
this river running through history,
this historical fact, this sweat
that put the aroma
in your choice Virginia,
that sweeten the cane
and make the cotton shine;
and sometimes I dream a nightmare
dream, that the river rising.
rising and swelling the sea
and I see you choking and drowning
in a sea of black man sweat
and I wake up shaking
with shame and remorse
for my mother did teach me,
"Child, don't study revenge."
Don't think we not grateful, boss,
how you cool down the place for we

comfort, but the line shuffle forward
one step at a time like Big Fraid hold we,
and the cool-cut, crew-cut Marine boy
wid him ice-blue eye and him walkie-talkie
dissa walk through the place and pretend
him no see we.
But a bring me handkerchief,
me mother did bring me up right,
and, God willing, I keeping things cool
till we meet face to face,
and I promise you, boss,
if I get through I gone,
gone from this bruk-spirit
kiss-me-arse place.

SOMETIMES IN THE MIDDLE OF THE STORY
(for the drowned Africans of the Middle Passage)

Sometimes in the middle of the story something
move outside the house, like
it could be the wind, but is not the wind
and the story-teller hesitate so slight
you hardly notice it, and the children
hold their breath and look at one another.
The old people say is Toussaint passing
on his grey horse Bel Argent, moving
faster than backra-massa timepiece
know to measure, briefing the captains
setting science and strategy to trap the emperor.
But also that sound had something in it
of deep water, salt water, had ocean,
the sleep-sigh of a drowned African
turning on his sleep on the ocean floor,
and Toussaint horse was coming from far
his tail trailing the swish of the sea
from secret rendezvous, from councils of war
with those who never completed the journey,
and we below deck heard only the muffled
thud of scuffling feet, could only
guess the quick, fierce tussle, the
stifled gasp, the barrel-chests bursting
the bubbles rising and breaking, the blue
closing over. But their souls shuttle
still the forest paths of ocean
connecting us still the current unbroken
the circuits kept open, the tireless messengers,
the ebony princes of your lost Atlantis,
a power of black men rising from the sea.

LIGNUM VITAE

When the final carry-down artist lock down
this town and scorch the earth till not
even lizard don't crawl, those who still living
next morning will see me surviving still,
wood of life, salvation tree,
I renew my phases of lilac-blue
and gold and always green. I am
a shady place for those who have lost
their way to the house of the man who gave
them stones for bread.
                            I don't want to sound
like I boasting, but too many small men in this two-
by-four place is giant, and you only have to open
your mouth and you can hang up a shingle outside
your gate with "expert" behind you name.
And to think, so many people born
and grow and dead and never feel
the rainbreeze blowing cool across

Cinchona from Catherine's Peak at middle
day. Sometimes I feel my heart
harden, but I not going nowhere, my root
sink too deep, and when the 8 o'clock sun
wake up the generations of stale pee and puke
that stain the sidewalk by Parade, I weep,
I bloom choirs of small butterflies.

A WAY OF GOING

He travelled light. At every stop
he shed impediments.
"Life is a casting off".
Counter-clerks, incredulous, peered
round queues, convinced
some piece of luggage was concealed.

When he arrived, eventually,
there was nothing to declare,
no bags for overworked officials to approve,
no guns, no gifts, no drugs,
nor precious stones, nor booze.
Free of desires and regrets and ideologies,
he walked into the night
and disappeared.

A RAIN-WASHED TOWN BY THE SEA

The scrunch of the kitchen knife through the long stalks
of ginger lilies I cut for my mother
this leaf-moist morning. Their sharp scent
pierces me.
             Way above the trumpet
tree, noisy with the gossip of birds,
improbably far, the silver stylus
of a jet chalks the arrow of my
ambition across immaculate blue.
Even as I gaze it dissolves in puff balls
of vapour.
             From my school desk, carved
with the names of the lost, the heroes, I shall dream
on the cobalt sea.
             By midday it will rain,
extravagantly, the gutters will gurgle with delight.

These memories define me. I keep them
against that morning when my eyes
no longer turn to greet the sun.

ABOUT THE AUTHOR

Edward Baugh is one of the Caribbean's major poets and a literary critic whose distinguished career has been devoted to West Indian literature – in particular to the work of Derek Walcott.

He was born in Jamaica in 1936. After completing a first degree at the University College of the West Indies, he pursued postgraduate research, and a Commonwealth Scholarship took him to the University of Manchester, where he gained a Ph.D. He taught at the University of the West Indies for well over thirty years. He has also held many visiting posts in America and the UK.

In a former life he was a talented actor and in later life the Public Orator at the University of the West Indies, Mona.